The Perfect Indian Barbecue

by Zahda Saeed

www.authenticindianfood.com

Photography and design by Kate Faxen

Contents

Preface   **6**

Introduction   **7**

Chapter 1: Shopping List   **9**

    Shopping list - Basic ingredients and equipment   10

Chapter 2: The Masala Method   **12**

    The masala method   13

Chapter 3: For the Barbecue   **14**

    Tandoori chicken   15

    Lamb kebabs   16

    Char-grilled spicy lamb chops   17

    Chilli and garlic prawns   17

Chapter 4: Vegetable Dishes   **19**

    Cauliflower and potato masala   20

    Okra masala   21

    Sweet and sour aubergine   22

    Aloo tikki   23

Chapter 5: Pulses (Daals)   **24**

    Tarka daal   25

    Spicy chickpea stir fry   26

    Chaana curry (chickpea)   27

Chapter 6: Chutneys, Yoghurt and Condiments   **28**

    Mint chutney (puthina)   29

    Tamarind and coriander chutney   29

    Cucumber raita   30

    Coriander and yoghurt   30

    Mint and yoghurt   31

    Onions and tomatoes in vinegar with red chillies (cachumbre)   31

Chapter 7: Rice   **32**

    Simple boiled rice   33

    Vegetable pilau rice   33

Chapter 8: Pudding   **35**

    Fruit chaat   36

Photography

Zahda Saeed   7

Chilli and garlic prawns, ready to go onto the barbecue   8

Fresh ingredients   9

Garam masala   9 & 11

Essential spices   11

The masala   12

Chilli and garlic prawns   14

Tandoori chicken kebabs   14

Lamb kebabs   16

Char-grilled spicy lamb chops   18

Sweet and sour aubergine   19

Aloo tikki   19

Cauliflower and potato masala   20

Okra masala   21

Spicy chickpea stir fry   24

Tarka daal   24

Spicy chickpea stir fry with raita   26

Chaana curry   27

Tamarind and coriander chutney, mint chutney and cucumber raita   28

Simple boiled rice   32

Vegetable pilau rice   34

Fruit chaat   35

NB: The images in this book have been taken without the use of a food stylist, in other words; all the food was prepared freshly by Zahda herself and photographed without using any trickery!

Preface

During the last thirty years the UK has witnessed three seminal developments in the world of cooking particularly in South Asian food. Indian and Pakistani dishes are now the nation's favourite cuisine, the "Indian" restaurant or cafe is to be seen on every high street throughout the land and there has been a media explosion in terms of cookery books and television programmes for all types of cuisine.

So why the need for yet another Indian cook book? What sets the philosophy and recipes in this book aside from others?

Well firstly, the aim of this book is to bring together two great British traditions: the summer barbecue and the love of Indian food. The dishes in this book are a constellation of ingredients, recipes and techniques handed down by word of mouth and hours of practice across 3 generations, originating in Northern India, Pakistan and ultimately in England. The dishes have been chosen to compliment each other and allow the reader to plan and successfully create a delicious Indian barbecue whether it be for a small or large gathering. Secondly, the recipes and style of cuisine counter one of the less desirable consequences of the last thirty years: the gradual Anglicisation of Asian food in the UK and the resultant dilution of the integrity of the original recipes.

Thirdly, this book emphasises the importance of fresh ingredients and how this is key to producing highly enjoyable dishes.

The clarity and simplicity of the recipes allows the reader to produce wonderful dishes consistently (south Asian dishes are still considered difficult to do well by many in the UK).

Finally, how do I know this? As Zahda's husband, I have enjoyed the fruits of her labour for the last 25 years and I strongly commend her recipes to you!

Shakeel R. Saeed

Introduction

My name is Zahda Saeed. I have been teaching Indian cookery classes for several years to numerous students from my home. People who come to my courses are amazed at how a combination of basic spices can produce such a wide variety of dishes. Many of my students have urged me to share my culinary delights with a wider audience. For this reason I am delighted to present a selection of my repertoire for those who wish to explore a different kind of barbecue. I have included basic techniques which can also be used in a wide range of curries so by mastering the few you will be a master of many!

The recipes I have selected for this book are authentic and healthy. With my food you will be able to taste the individual spices, their fusion and their exotic flavours.

All spices used are obtainable from most local supermarkets and your local Indian store at very reasonable prices.

Enjoy!

Chapter 1: Shopping List

Shopping list - Basic ingredients & equipment

Onions

Avoid buying sweet tasting onions (such as English) as these tend to give the curry an overly sweet taste. Dutch or Spanish onions are recommended.

Oil

Traditionally ghee (clarified butter) is used but this is high in saturated fats which are to be avoided in healthy diets and so I have replaced them with oils such as corn oil or olive oil. Rapeseed oil is better still for your heart!

Fresh coriander

This belongs to the same family as parsley and is used to season a curry at the end of cooking. The fruit (seeds) are widely used as condiments with or without roasting in the preparation of curry powders and seasonings.

Garlic

Only a little is used as it will mask the flavour of the food.

Chillies

As a rule the thinner they are the stronger or hotter they are. Green chillies become red as they ripen. Both green and red chillies may be equally hot, the red ones having a sweeter more rounded flavour.

Tomatoes

These can be tinned or fresh. They give the curry tanginess and add a rich colour to the dish.

Spices

Turmeric, red chilli powder, salt, ground garam masala, ground cumin powder, dried pomegranate seeds, dried mango powder, saffron strands, panch puran (which is made up of fennel seeds, mustard seeds, nigella (onion) seeds, fenugreek seeds and cumin seeds), black rock salt.

Garam masala

The garam masala can be used ground or whole and consists of: cinnamon sticks, green cardamoms, black cardamoms, cloves, cumin seeds, coriander seeds and bay leaves (see below).

To make 100g of ground garam masala add a 3cm cinnamon stick to 5 green cardamoms, 8 black cardamoms, 5 black cloves, 2 tbsp of cumin seeds, 2 tbsp coriander seeds and 4 bay leaves.

I use a coffee grinder in which I place whole ingredients and grind until a fine powder is formed. This only takes a few seconds and will last up to a month in an airtight container.

Garam masala (centre) is made from the ingredients described and shown here.

I assure you that making your own garam masala will make that extra bit of difference when preparing your Indian dishes.

Essential spices: clockwise from top right – red chilli powder, turmeric, salt, garam masala, cumin and coriander powder in the centre.

Equipment

A heavy bottomed pan is required, one in which food can be left to cook on a slow heat. Curries can be cooked on all different types of cooking appliances (even Agas, I am informed by my students).

If you would like to try mixing your own spices you can use a pestle and mortar or cheat (like I do) by using a coffee grinder.

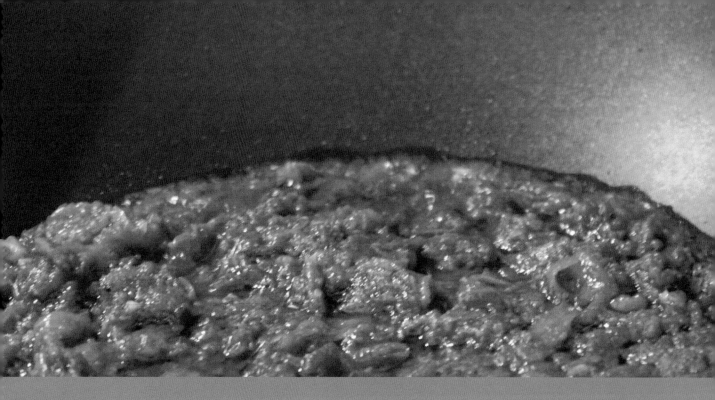

Chapter 2: The Masala Method

The masala method

The masala method is the basic recipe used to cook a whole range of dishes such as vegetables, pulses, meat, cheese and seafood. Once you've mastered this versatile technique you really should be able to turn almost any ingredient into a satisfying and flavoursome dish. Although it can take up to 40 to 60 minutes to prepare, once you have it, you may freeze it or you may keep it in the fridge for up to 10 days.

Ingredients

- 3 medium sized onions, peeled and chopped
- 7 tbsp cooking oil
- 5 cloves of garlic, whole, peeled
- 1 cm fresh root ginger, grated
- 1 green chilli, finely chopped
- 1 plum tomato, chopped
- ½ a bunch of fresh coriander, chopped

Spices

- 1 tsp salt
- 1 tsp red chilli powder
- ¼ tsp turmeric powder
- 3 tsp coriander powder
- 1 tsp garam masala

Method

1. Sweat the onions and garlic in oil for 30-45 minutes until slightly golden and then mash with a large stirring spoon.

2. Add all the spices, tomato and half the ginger to this mixture and cook on a high heat for 5 minutes stirring to prevent the mixture burning and sticking. If it does stick then add splashes of water and stir. You should now have a golden brown paste where the onions have dissolved and the oil has separated out. This is the Masala. The other half of the ginger and green chillies should be added later (see individual recipes).

Chapter 3: For the Barbecue

Tandoori chicken

Ingredients

- 1 whole chicken, jointed, cut into 8 – 10 pieces
- Juice of 1 lemon

Marinade

- 1 tbsp of cooking oil
- 3 tbsp of natural yoghurt
- 1 tsp of garlic powder
- 1 dsp salt
- 1 dsp chilli powder
- 1 dsp coriander powder
- 1 tsp garam masala
- Pinch of cumin seeds
- ¼ tsp of egg yellow powder (optional as yellow food colouring)

Method

1. Place the chicken pieces in a bowl with all the lemon juice and salt. Allow to stand for 10 minutes.

2. In a separate bowl prepare the marinade: place the yoghurt in the bowl and add the oil and all the spices.

3. Add the marinade to the chicken and allow to stand in the fridge for at least 1 hour – the longer the chicken is marinated the tastier it will be.

4. Thread smaller chicken pieces onto skewers or place larger pieces directly onto the barbecue and turn regularly. (Alternatively place on a baking tray and bake in a preheated oven (gas mark 6) for 40 to 45 minutes.)

5. Tandoori chicken may be served as an accompaniment to a meal or as a starter with chutney and salad.

Lamb kebabs

Ingredients

- 1lb (454g) lamb mince (from leg if possible)
- ½ large bunch of coriander
- 1 small onion
- 2 green chillies
- 1 egg
- Oil for shallow frying

Spices

- 1 tsp salt
- 1 tsp garam masala
- ½ tsp red chilli powder
- 1 tsp anardana (dried pomegranate seed)
- 1 clove garlic
- 1cm fresh root ginger
- 1 tsp cumin powder
- 1 tsp coriander powder

Method

1. Place the onion, green chillies, coriander, garlic, ginger and egg in the blender and blend until finely chopped.

2. Add half the minced lamb and the rest of the spices and blend for 30 seconds.

3. Put the blended lamb with the rest of the lamb in a large bowl and mix.

4. Shape into kebabs or small burgers – these are ready for the barbecue.

Char-grilled spicy lamb chops

Ingredients

- 12 medium sized lamb chops
- 1 tsp chilli powder
- 1 tbsp salt
- 2 tbsp malt vinegar
- 3 tsp coriander powder
- 1 tsp garam masala
- 2 tbsp plain yoghurt

Method

1. Make the marinade by adding all the spices to the yoghurt and the vinegar.

2. Next add the chops to the marinade and mix well. Leave to stand for a minimum of 2 hours but preferably overnight in the fridge.

3. Cook to taste on the barbecue.

Chilli and garlic prawns

Ingredients

- 12 fresh or frozen raw tiger prawns (this recipe also works for barbecued king prawns or fish such as tuna or monkfish)

Marinade

- 1 tsp salt
- ½ tsp red chilli powder
- 1 clove garlic
- 1 cm fresh root ginger
- 1 tbsp olive oil
- 2 tbsp lemon juice

Method

1. Mix all the marinade ingredients in a bowl.

2. Add the prawns (or fish) and leave for 20 minutes.

3. Place the prawns onto skewers – you can also add cut vegetables such as peppers and tomatoes. These are now ready to barbecue.

Chapter 4: Vegetable Dishes

Cauliflower and potato masala

Ingredients

▷ Masala ingredients (see page 13)

▷ 3 large potatoes, peeled and chopped into small pieces

▷ 1 medium cauliflower, chopped or 1 large aubergine, chopped (or any vegetable of your choice)

▷ ½ a bunch of fresh coriander, chopped

Method

1. First make the masala curry base as decribed on page 13.

2. Add the chopped vegetables to the masala with the second half of the ginger (left over from the masala method) and ¼ cup of water. Bring to the boil then turn down the heat and allow to cook on a low heat until the vegetables are cooked (approx 15 minutes).

3. Add the coriander and green chillies (from the masala method) mix in and serve.

Okra masala

Ingredients

- Masala ingredients (see page 13)
- 500g of fresh okra, chopped into quarters
- ½ a bunch of fresh coriander, chopped

Method

1. First make the masala curry base as decribed on page 13.

2. Add the okra pieces to the masala with the second half of the ginger (left over from the masala method) and ¼ cup of water. Bring to the boil then turn down the heat and allow to cook on a low heat until the vegetables are cooked (approx 15 minutes).

3. Add the coriander and green chillies (from the masala method) mix in and serve.

Sweet and sour aubergine
(a Gujarati variation of vegetable masala)

Ingredients

- Masala ingredients (see page 13)
- 1 large aubergine or 6 baby aubergines, whole
- 1 dsp panch pooran (Asian 5 spice)
- 200g tamarind
- 1 standard teacup of sugar (approximately 240g)
- 5 tbsp fresh coriander, chopped

Method

1. First make the tamarind sauce

   a) Place the tamarind in 250ml of water and soak for 2 hours.

   b) Sieve to make a watery sauce.

2. Next make the masala curry base as described on page 13.

3. Add the panch pooran with the second half of the ginger (left over from the masala method) to the masala and stir.

4. Add the tamarind sauce and the sugar to the masala and cook for 3-5 minutes.

5. Make several slits along the aubergine(s). Deep-fry the aubergine(s) whole in a pan for about 5 minutes or until they begin to wrinkle. If you don't want to deep-fry you can brush the aubergine with oil, wrap in foil and bake in a medium oven for 50 minutes.

6. Add the aubergine to the masala and cook for 5 minutes.

7. Mix in the green chillies (from the masala method) and garnish with the fresh coriander.

Aloo tikki

Ingredients

- 1 small onion, chopped or bunch of spring onions, chopped
- 5-6 medium potatoes
- 1 green chilli
- 5 tbsp fresh coriander, chopped
- 1 egg, beaten
- Cooking oil for shallow frying

Spices

- ¼ tsp of chilli powder
- 1 tsp pomegranate seeds, crushed
- ½ tsp of garam masala
- 1 tsp of salt

Method

1. Boil and mash the potatoes coarsely but do not add milk and butter.

2. To the mash add the onions, green chilli, coriander and all the spices. Mix well.

3. Form into 12 tikkis (small patties).

4. Dip into the beaten egg taking care not to break up the tikkis.

5. Shallow fry until golden brown (about 2 minutes on either side).

Chapter 5: Pulses (Daals)

Tarka daal

Ingredients

- 50g butter
- 400g of red split lentils (you can also use green or brown lentils, black eyed beans or yellow split peas)
- Water
- 3 tbsp fresh coriander, chopped
- 4 cloves of garlic, finely chopped
- 3cm fresh root ginger, grated
- 2 green chillies, 1 left whole, 1 chopped.

Spices

- 1 tsp salt
- 1 tsp red chilli powder
- ¼ tsp turmeric powder

Method

1. Wash and soak the lentils for between 10 minutes and 1hour (the longer the better).

2. Drain off the water and place the lentils in large pan (without spices). Cover with water so that the water rises 2cm above the lentils.

3. Bring to the boil and add all the spices and one whole green chilli.

4. Reduce the heat and simmer gently for 10-15 minutes until the lentils are cooked. To test, squeeze a lentil between your finger and thumb; if the lentil mashes up quickly then they are cooked.

5. Next, mash up some of the lentils with a spoon so that the mixture becomes creamy. Add all the coriander.

6. Switch off the heat and make the tarka:

   a) Melt the butter in a pan with a splash of oil to stop it burning. Add the finely chopped garlic, grated ginger and chopped chilli.

   b) Stir the mixture constantly until the garlic becomes golden brown (take care not to burn the garlic).

7. Add this to the daal and serve.

Spicy chickpea stir fry

Ingredients

- ▷ 1 fresh tomato, sliced
- ▷ 1 small potato, chopped and cooked (optional)
- ▷ ¼ green pepper, sliced
- ▷ 1 small onion, finely chopped
- ▷ 1 green chilli, chopped
- ▷ Lemon juice (to season)
- ▷ 1 tbsp olive oil
- ▷ 1 tin of cooked chickpeas (400g)

Spices

- ▷ 1 tsp channa masala
- ▷ 1 tsp jeera powder
- ▷ 1 tsp dhania powder
- ▷ ¾ tsp salt
- ▷ ¼ tsp turmeric
- ▷ ¼ tsp whole jeera seeds

Method

1. Heat oil in a pan and add the whole jeera seeds, allow them to start spitting then add the rest of the spices.

2. Now add the chickpeas to the spices and cook for 2 minutes.

3. Add the rest of the vegetables (including the potato if using) and the coriander and stir fry for another 2 minutes. Add a squeeze of lemon juice, mix and eat!

As a serving suggestion, why not add a dollop of homemade cucumber raita!

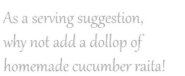

Chaana curry (chickpea)

Ingredients

▷ Masala ingredients (see page 13)

▷ 1 tin of cooked chickpeas (400g)

Method

1. Prepare the masala as described on page 13.

2. Drain the chickpeas, wash thoroughly and add them to the masala together with the other half of the ginger (left over from the masala method) and 1½ cups of water.

3. Cook on a high heat until cooking vigorously and cover the pan with a lid and cook for a further 20 minutes until the chickpeas become mushy.

4. Mix in the green chillies (from the masala method) and serve.

Chapter 6: Chutneys, Yoghurt and Condiments

Mint chutney (puthina)

Ingredients

- 2 whole green chillies
- 5 dsp of fresh mint, chopped
- Juice of 2 whole lemons
- 1 tsp of sugar
- 1 tsp of salt

Method

1. Place all the ingredients in a blender and pulse until a smooth paste-like chutney is formed.

Tamarind and coriander chutney

Ingredients

- 200g of wet tamarind
- 600ml water
- ½ a large onion
- 3 whole green chillies
- 1 tsp salt
- 1 tsp sugar
- 5 dsp coriander, chopped
- ½ tsp chilli powder
- 1cm root ginger, cut into cubes

Method

1. Place the tamarind in the water and soak for 2 hours.

2. Sieve the tamarind to make a sauce.

3. Place the tamarind sauce in a blender with all the other ingredients and blend until the desired texture is reached (fine or coarse).

Cucumber raita

Ingredients

- 425g of natural yoghurt
- Milk or water (as required)
- ½ a small cucumber
- ¼ tsp cumin seeds
- ¼ tsp black pepper
- Salt (to taste)

Method

1. Place the yoghurt in a bowl and add the spices.

2. Grate the cucumber and add it to the yoghurt.

3. Stir and check the consistency. If the yoghurt is too thick, thin by adding milk or water.

Coriander and yoghurt

Ingredients

- 1 whole green chilli
- 5 tbsp of fresh coriander
- 200g natural yoghurt
- Water (as required)
- ¼ tsp salt
- ¼ tsp garam masala
- ¼ whole onion, roughly chopped
- Red chilli powder (to taste)

Method

1. Place coriander, chilli and onion in a blender with 2 tbsp yoghurt and blend.

2. Add this mixture to the rest of the yoghurt and add salt, garam masala and chilli powder.

3. If the mixture is too thick, thin with water.

Mint and yoghurt

Ingredients

- 1 whole green chilli
- 5 dsp of fresh mint, chopped
- 200g natural yoghurt
- Water (as required)
- ¼ tsp salt
- ¼ tsp garam masala
- ¼ whole onion
- Red chilli powder (to taste)

Method

1. Place the mint, chilli and onion in a blender with 2 tablespoons of yoghurt and blend.

2. Add this mixture to the rest of the yoghurt and add salt, garam masala and chilli powder.

3. If the mixture is too thick, thin with water.

Onions and tomatoes in vinegar with red chillies (cachumbre)

Ingredients

- 1 small onion
- 2 tomatoes
- 4 tbsp of malt vinegar
- ½ tsp of salt
- ½ tsp of red chilli powder

Method

1. Dice the onion and tomatoes and then add the vinegar and spices.

2. Mix and serve.

Chapter 7: Rice

Simple boiled rice (serves 4)

Ingredients

- 800g (2 medium sized glasses) of basmati long grain rice
- Water
- 1 tsp salt
- 1 tbsp cooking oil

Method

1. Wash and soak rice – minimum of ½ hr, for best results 1 hr.

2. Bring a large pan of water to the boil approximately ½ - ¾ full. Add 1 tsp of salt and 1 tbsp of cooking oil.

3. Next add the rice to the water and bring back to boil and simmer until rice is cooked al dente (roughly 5 minutes).

4. Drain rice and place back in pan and steam on a very low heat for 15 minutes.

Vegetable pilau rice (serves 6)

Ingredients

- 2 large onions
- 8 cloves of garlic, peeled but left whole
- 1200g (3 medium sized glasses) of basmati long grain rice
- 250g butter
- 2 cups of frozen peas, or cooked chick peas * (see over page)
- 3 ¾ glasses of water** (see over page)

Spices

- 2 dsp cumin seed
- 4 black cardamoms
- 1 tbsp salt
- 2 dsp coriander seeds
- 3-4 cinnamon sticks
- 4 cloves
- 4cm fresh root ginger, grated

Method

1. Wash and soak the rice for 1 hour prior to cooking.

2. Melt the butter in a large pan.

3. Slice the onions (not too finely) and add to the melted butter with the garlic cloves. Cook on a low heat for 40-45 minutes until caramelised.

4. Add all the spices and cook on a high heat for 1 minute.

5. Now add the vegetables and cook on a high heat for a further 2 minutes.

6. Add 3¾ glasses of water to the pan and bring to the boil. Add the rice at this stage. Once boiling again turn down to a medium heat and allow the rice to cook. When the rice has absorbed most of the water, turn the heat right down to the lowest setting and cover. Allow to cook for a further 15-20 minutes.

* (From previous page) at this stage you can also add prawns, cooked chicken or cooked chick peas.

** (From previous page) always add 1¼ glasses of water for each 1 glass of rice.

Chapter 8: Pudding

Fruit chaat (serves 6)

This is the ideal refreshing summer dessert to accompany the barbecue.

Ingredients

- 2 medium sized bananas
- 1 large red apple
- ½ tin (200g) of guava in syrup (2 fresh chopped guava may also be used)
- ½ tin (250g) of lychees in syrup (10 fresh peeled lychees may also be used)
- Seeds from half of a pomegranate
- 250ml of tinned mango pulp

Method

1. Chop the apple and bananas into small slices.

2. Add all the fruit to the mango pulp.

3. Stir gently.

4. Chill in the fridge for 1 hour.

This may also be served with vanilla ice-cream.

Index

Aloo tikki	–	23	Mint chutney (puthina) –	29
Cachumbre	–	31	Okra masala –	21
Cauliflower and potato masala	–	20	Shopping list –	10
Chaana curry (chickpea)	–	27	Simple boiled rice –	33
Char-grilled spicy lamb chops	–	17	Spicy chickpea stir fry –	26
Chilli and garlic prawns	–	17	Sweet and sour aubergine –	22
Coriander and yoghurt	–	30	Tamarind and coriander chutney –	29
Cucumber raita	–	30	Tandoori chicken –	15
Fruit chaat	–	36	Tarka daal –	25
Lamb kebabs	–	16	The masala method –	13
Mint and yoghurt	–	31	Vegetable pilau rice –	33

Made in the USA
Charleston, SC
09 September 2013